This book belongs to:

_____

In remembrance of my grandparents Virginia, Ernest, Annie, Jessie, and all my ancestors known and unknown.

For my children Efosa, Esosa, and all future generations.

Sankofa.

Copyright © 2020 Jessica Ann Mitchell Aiwuyor
All rights reserved. This book or any portion thereof may not
be reproduced or used in any manner whatsoever
without the express written permission of the publisher
except for the use of brief quotations in a book review.

Written by Jessica Ann Mitchell Aiwuyor
Cover Design and Illustrations by Chasity Hampton
Additional Illustrations by GraphicsFactory.com.

ISBN 978-1-948061-08-7

Published by Our Legaci Press, LLC

Printed in the United States of America

First Printing, 2020

OurLegaciPress.com

Annie was having a **ROUGH** week!

It all started on Monday when
her shoelaces became untied at school.

She tripped over them and fell flat on her
face in front of everyone.

On Tuesday, Annie was drinking chocolate milk and spilled it all over her white sweater.

This happened right before her turn to take yearbook pictures.

OF COURSE...

Her brother Leroy and sister Mae thought it was quite hilarious.

Wednesday was just as **FRUSTRATING**.

Annie lost her favorite hair bow and had to wear the big puffy one that she hated.

Now, it was Thursday.
Annie was excited because she planned to present her favorite toy in class.

She was all set to bring Mrs. Suzie Q,, a teddy bear that her grandmother helped her hand sew.

However, when it was Annie's turn to present her special teddy bear, it wasn't in her book bag. That's when she remembered that she accidentally left it on the kitchen table.

Poor Annie couldn't seem to catch a break.
When she came home from school,
Annie picked up her teddy bear and sighed.

"Humph," she said as she sat down
at the kitchen table next to Mae and Leroy.

"What's got you in a pickle?"
Mae asked.

I feel like I can't do anything right. Every day this week something bad has happened," Annie said.

Then, she told her family about all of the week's misfortunes.

"Ahhhh, looks like you need
five black-eyed peas," Pops replied.

"Five black-eyed peas?
What's that going to do?"
Annie asked.

Then, Pops told Annie his story.

"When I was a little boy, I had a
very rough week just like you.
Nothing seemed to be going right,"
said Pops.

"I broke my only pair of glasses.
My favorite toy soldier disappeared.
One of my bicycle's pedals fell off

AND...
I forgot to bring my homework to school."

"My mama's mama told
me not to worry.

She said all I needed was
five black-eyed peas.

But Ma'dear how will that help?,
I asked.

'Well,' she said.
'Don't you worry about how it
works and just know that it does.'

With that, Ma'dear took me to her
super-secret special garden," said Pops.

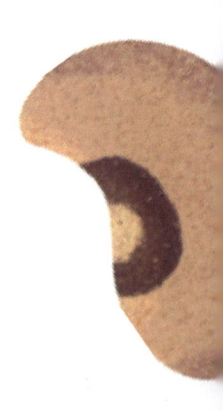

"Ma'dear had every herb and spice you could think of, including a few secret ones."

"She grabbed a little bit of this and a little bit of that.

She took all of the ingredients and boiled them in a pot with just five black-eyed peas."

"Before I knew it, those little peas swelled up as big as potatoes.

Each one of the them did something special.

One pea was for strength.

One pea was for confidence.

One pea was for faith.

One pea was for happiness.

And one pea was to remember her mama's mama that taught her the five black-eyed peas recipe."

"Those five black-eyed peas were so big, that I wasn't sure if I could finish them," Pops said.

"You couldn't tell me anything.
I was the large and in-charge master chef!"
exclaimed Pops.

"The next day, I still couldn't find my toy.
My glasses were still broken. Yet, it didn't
matter because now I had the secret of the
five black-eyed peas."

"I knew that no matter what happened,
I would be unstoppable," said Pops.

Annie's eyes grew wide.
"Pops," She said.

"Will you teach me the recipe?
Will you make me the five
black-eyed peas?" she asked.

"Me too!" shouted Leroy.

"Me too!" yelled Mae.

Pops turned around with
a sly grin on his face and said,
"Babies, you already know the recipe.
You just don't know that you know."

Then, Pops took Annie, Leroy, and Mae to his super-secret special garden.

He let them pick a little bit of this
and a little bit of that.

Together, they poured the ingredients into a big pot with five black-eyed peas that grew to the size of potatoes.

Their plates were filled to the brim.

"Well, youngin. The five black-eyed peas are a super-secret Sanders family recipe," said Pops.

It's been our family recipe since
before people started driving cars.
It's something we just know how to do.

But every one has a gift.

Your gift makes you unique.
You know how to make this recipe.

However, your friends can do
other things that make them special,"
Pops explained.

The next day Annie had a
big grin on her face.

It didn't matter that she spilled
chocolate milk or wore a silly bow.
It didn't matter that she forgot her teddy bear.

She couldn't stop smiling because
she knew the family recipe for
five black-eyed peas.

If she could make that,
what else could she make?

What else could she do?

By using her heart, her mind,
and a little bit of this with a little bit of that...

Annie felt
INVINCIBLE.

And she was!

CPSIA information can be obtained
at www.ICGtesting.com
Printed in the USA
BVHW011736230223
659101BV00016B/63